Editor
Sara Connolly

Illustrator
Kelly McMahon

Cover Artist
Barb Lorseyedi

Managing Editor
Ina Massler Levin, M.A.

Creative Director
Karen J. Goldfluss, M.S. Ed.

Art Production Manager
Kevin Barnes

Art Coordinator
Renée Christine Yates

Imaging
Nathan P. Rivera

Publisher
Mary D. Smith, M.S. Ed.

MAKING WORDS

Author

Jessica M. Dubin Kissel, M.A.

Teacher Created Resources, Inc.
6421 Industry Way
Westminster, CA 92683
www.teachercreated.com
ISBN: 978-1-4206-8614-2

© 2007 Teacher Created Resources, Inc.
Made in U.S.A.

Table of Contents

Table of Contents

Introduction

Flipping Over Making Words is a supplemental series designed for helping emergent readers. Templates are provided for teachers to make student flip books to actively show how words can be manipulated by changing a letter or series of letters.

Flip books provide a wonderful opportunity to tap into kinesthetic learners. Kinesthetic learners will thrive as they get to use their hands to flip pages in order to make words. Flip books also allow students to make words without the frustrations that are connected with writing words using pencil and paper. Furthermore, flip books give every student the opportunity to be actively involved in making words at the same time.

Following each flip book is a word list, activity ideas for teachers, and student handouts. The activities were written to be age appropriate and to help develop students' reading and writing skills. Best of all, these activities are meant to be motivational and fun.

Teachers can use the materials provided, create their own activities using the flip books and word lists, or simply call out words on the list and ask the students to make those words.

This series is not a reading program. This series was designed so that teachers can pull active and interesting activities into their lessons as instructional aids and as follow-up practice. Teachers should not feel like they need to use the activities in any particular order.

Variations on Making Flip Books

Templates are provided so that teachers can easily make flip books for each individual student using nothing more than paper, scissors, and staples. However, there are other ways that the flip books can be made and used in the classroom. Here are some other ideas:

- Make a flip book for a group of students to use together.

- Make one large flip book to use as a class.

- Use rings or plastic spiral binders instead of staples.

- Once the flip book is stapled, separate the different columns so that the flip book is no longer one unit. Have different students be responsible for different parts of the flip book.

- Use different colored paper.

- Put a row of blank squares on the top of the flip book. Have the students illustrate them.

- Laminate the flip books or use cardstock to make them sturdy.

- Have the students cut out their own flip books to develop fine motor skills.

- Distribute blank flip books and have the students fill in the letters using their own writing.

- Have students trace the letters with glue and add glitter.

Cautionary Note: Please be advised that while using the flip books, there is always the possibility that undesirable or unexpected words can be formed. Such words are not included in the word lists.

Standards and Benchmarks

Listed below are the McREL standards for Languange Arts, Level 1 (grades K–2). All standards and benchmarks are used with permission from McREL.

Kendall, J. S., & Marzano R. J. (2004). *Content knowledge: A compendium of standards and benchmarks for K–12 education.* Aurora, CO: Mid-continent Research for Education and Learning. Online database:

http://www.mcrel.org/standards-benchmarks/

McREL Standards are in **bold**. Benchmarks are in regular print. The ideas and activities throughout this book meet the following standards and benchmarks. The page numbers for the correlating handouts are listed to the right.

3. Uses grammatical and mechanical conventions in written compositions

Uses conventions of print in writing (e.g., forms letters in print, uses upper- and lowercase letters of the alphabet, spaces words and sentences, writes from left-to-right and top-to-bottom)	14–18, 28–31, 40–43, 53–62, 74–77, 83–86, 94–100, 109, 111–112, 120–122, 133–136, 142–149, 159–163, 173–176
Uses conventions of spelling in written compositions (e.g., spells high frequency, commonly misspelled words from appropriate grade-level list; spells phonetically regular words; uses letter-sound relationships; spells basic short vowel, long vowel, r-controlled, and consonant blend patterns)	14–18, 28–31, 40–43, 53–62, 74–77, 83–86, 94–100, 109–112, 120–122, 133–136, 142–149, 159–163, 173–176

5. Uses the general skills and strategies of the reading process

Uses basic elements of phonetic analysis (e.g., common letter/sound relationships, beginning and ending consonants, vowel sounds, blends, word patterns) to decode unknown words	14–18, 28, 30–31, 40–43, 53–62, 71, 73–77, 83–86, 94–100, 109, 111–112, 120–125, 133–136, 142–149, 159–163, 173–176
Uses basic elements of structural analysis (e.g., syllables, basic prefixes, suffixes, root words, spelling patterns) to decode unknown words	14–18, 22, 28, 31, 40–43, 53–62, 71–77, 83–86, 94–100, 109–110, 112, 120–125, 133–136, 142–149, 159–176
Understands level-appropriate sight words and vocabulary (e.g., words for persons, places, things, actions; high frequency words such as *said*, *was*, and *where*)	14–18, 28, 30–31, 40–43, 53–62, 71–77, 83–86, 94, 96–100, 109, 111–112, 120–125, 133–136, 142–149, 159–163, 173–176

8. Uses listening and speaking strategies for different purposes

Makes contributions in class and group discussions (e.g., initiates conversations, connects ideas and experiences with those of others)	96–100, 123–125
Asks and responds to questions (e.g., about the meaning of a story, about the meaning of words or ideas)	71–73, 123–125
Follows rules of conversation and group discussion (e.g., takes turns, raises hand to speak, stays on topic, focuses attention on speaker)	71–73, 96–100, 123–125
Uses different voice level, phrasing, and intonation for different situations (e.g., small group settings, informal discussions, reports to the class)	14–18, 28, 30–31, 40–43, 53–62, 74–77, 83–84, 86, 94, 96–100, 109–110, 112, 120–125, 133–136, 142–149, 159–163, 173–176
Uses level-appropriate vocabulary in speech (e.g., number words; words that describe people, places, things, events, location, actions; synonyms, antonyms; homonyms)	14–18, 28, 30–31, 40–43, 53–62, 74–77, 83–84, 86, 94, 96–100, 109–110, 112, 120–125, 133–136, 142–148, 149, 159, 160, 161, 162, 163, 173, 174, 175, 176
Gives and responds to oral directions	All

Short A Flip Book

Directions: Make a flip book for each of your students.

1. Copy pages 6–9.
2. Cut the strips out horizontally along the outside dashed lines.
3. Cut along the vertical dashed lines in between the letters, not on the solid lines.
4. Stack the strips on top of each other and staple them together where the staple marks are indicated.

staple	staple
b	ag

staple	staple
c	at

Short A Flip Book *(cont.)*

staple	staple
h	an

staple	staple
l	ap

staple	staple
m	

Short A Flip Book *(cont.)*

staple	staple
p	

staple	staple
r	

staple	staple
s	

Short A Flip Book *(cont.)*

staple	staple
t	

staple	staple
w	

Short A Word List

Listed below are some words that can be made using the Short A Flip Book.

bag hag lag	hat mat pat	ran tan cap
rag sag tag	rat sat ban	lap map rap
wag bat cat	can man pan	sap tap

Activity Ideas for Teachers

The following activities can be used with the Short A Flip Book. Many of the activities have supporting materials. If the activities have supporting materials, the page numbers where the materials can be found will be provided.

Fun Hats

Directions:

1. Distribute the handout on page 14.
2. Instruct the students to work individually, in pairs, or in groups to complete the handout.
3. Explain to the students that they should use their flip books to help them finish the words inside of the hats.
4. Then, ask the students to circle the hat that they like the best.
5. Have the students practice reading the words that they wrote.

Answer Key: Answers may include:

bat, cat, hat, mat, pat, rat, sat

Play Ball

Directions:

1. Distribute the handout on page 15.
2. Instruct the students to work individually, in pairs, or in groups to complete the handout.
3. Explain to the students that the bat on the page can only hit balls that end with the letters *at*. Ask the student to use their flip books to help them finish the words inside of the baseballs.
4. Have the students practice reading the words that they wrote.

Answer Key: Answers may include:

bat, cat, hat, mat, pat, rat, sat

Activity Ideas for Teachers *(cont.)*

=============================== **Tags** ===============================

Directions:

1. Distribute the handout on page 16.
2. Instruct the students to work individually, in pairs, or in groups to complete the handout.
3. Explain to the students that they should use their flip books to help them finish the words inside of the tags.
4. Then, ask the students to circle the words that rhyme with *tag*.
5. Have the students practice reading the words that they wrote.

Answer Key: Answers may include:

(bag), (hag), (lag), (rag), (sag), (tag), (wag)

bat, cat, hat, mat, pat, rat, sat

ban, can, man, pan, ran, tan

cap, lap, map, rap, sap, tap

=============================== **Windy Words** ===============================

Directions:

1. Distribute the handout on page 17.
2. Instruct the students to work individually, in pairs, or in groups to complete the handout.
3. Explain to the students that they should use their flip books to help them finish the words before the fan blows them away.
4. Then, ask the students to circle the words that rhyme with *fan*.
5. Have the students practice reading the words that they wrote.

Answer Key: Answers may include:

bag, hag, lag, rag, sag, tag, wag

bat, cat, fat, hat, mat, pat, rat, sat

(ban), (can), (fan), (man), (pan), (ran), (tan)

cap, lap, map, rap, sap, tap

Activity Ideas for Teachers *(cont.)*

Hot Words

Directions:

1. Distribute the handout on page 18.
2. Instruct the students to work individually, in pairs, or in groups to complete the handout.
3. Explain to the students that they should use their flip books to help them finish the words inside of the pans.
4. Then, ask the students to place an X over the words that do not rhyme with *pan*.
5. Have the students practice reading the words that they wrote.

Answer Key: Answers may include:

ban, can, fan, man, pan, ran, tan

cap, lap, map, rap, sap, tap

bat, cat, fat, hat, mat, pat, rat, sat

Fun Hats

Directions: Use your flip books to help you finish the words inside each hat.
Then, circle the hat that you like best.

14

Play Ball

Directions: This bat can only hit balls that end with the letters *at*. Use your flip books to help you finish the words inside of the baseballs.

Tags

Directions: Use your flip books to help you complete the word that is written on each tag. Then, circle the words that rhyme with *tag*.

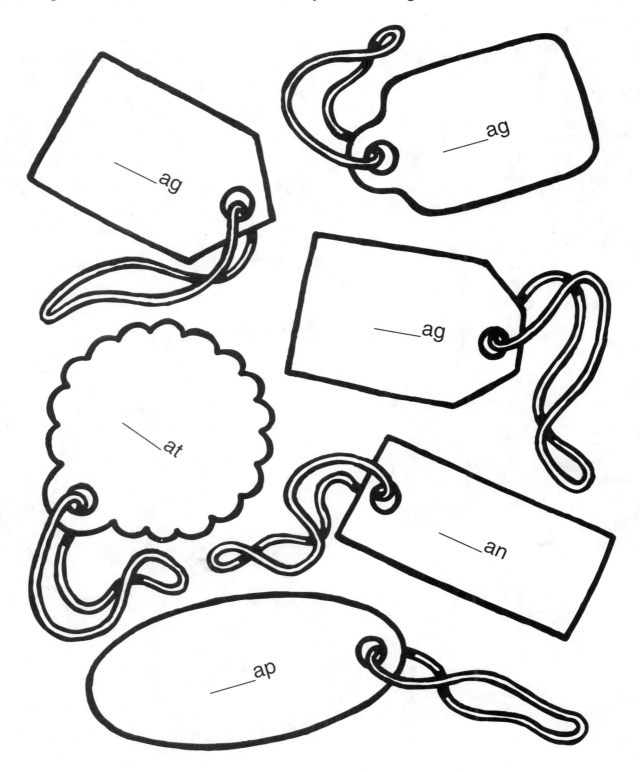

Windy Words

Directions: Help finish these words before the fan blows them away! Use your flip books to help you. Then, circle the words that rhyme with *fan*.

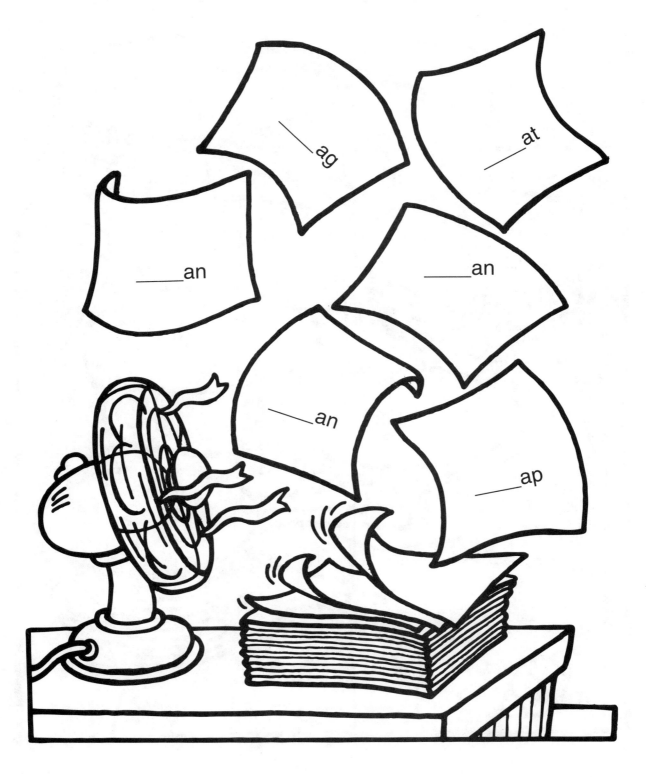

Hot Words

Directions: Use your flip books to help you finish the words inside of the pan. Place an **X** over the words that do not rhyme with *pan*.

18

Short E Flip Book

Directions: Make a flip book for each of your students.

1. Copy pages 19–24.

2. Cut the strips out horizontally, using the dotted lines as a guide.

3. Staple the strips together where the staple marks are indicated.

4. Cut the boxes vertically, cutting only on the dotted lines. Make sure not to separate the squares at the top.

staple	staple
b	ed

staple	staple
d	eg

Short E Flip Book *(cont.)*

staple	staple
f	en

staple	staple
g	et

staple	staple
h	

20

Short E Flip Book *(cont.)*

staple	staple
j	

staple	staple
l	

staple	staple
m	

Short E Flip Book *(cont.)*

staple	staple
n	

staple	staple
p	

staple	staple
r	

Short E Flip Book *(cont.)*

staple	staple
S	

staple	staple
t	

staple	staple
V	

Short E Flip Book *(cont.)*

staple	staple
W	

Short E Word List

Listed below are some words that can be made using the Short E Flip Book.

bed fed led	led peg den	ten bet get	net pet set
red wed beg	hen men pen	jet let met	vet wet

Activity Ideas for Teachers

The following activities can be used with the Short E Flip Book. Many of the activities have supporting materials. If the activities have supporting materials, the page numbers where the materials can be found will be provided.

―――――――――――――――――――――― **Caught in a Net** ――――――――――――――――――――――

Directions:

1. Distribute the handout on page 28.
2. Instruct the students to work individually, in pairs, or in groups to complete the handout.
3. Explain to the students that they should use their flip books to help them finish the words caught inside of the net.
4. Then, ask the students to circle the words that rhyme with *net*.
5. Have the students practice reading the words that they wrote.

Answer Key: Answers may include:

$\left(bet\right)$, $\left(get\right)$, $\left(jet\right)$, $\left(let\right)$, $\left(net\right)$, $\left(pet\right)$, $\left(set\right)$, $\left(vet\right)$, $\left(wet\right)$

beg, leg, peg

―――――――――――――――――――――――――――― **Eggs** ――――――――――――――――――――――――――――

Directions:

1. Distribute the handout on page 29.
2. Instruct the students to work individually, in pairs, or in groups to complete the handout.
3. Explain to the students that they should use their flip books to help them finish the words inside of the eggs.
4. Then, have the students draw lines from the mother hen to the words that rhyme with *hen*.
5. Have the students practice reading the words that they wrote.

Answer Key: Answers will vary. See The Short E Word List for possible answers.

26

Activity Ideas for Teachers *(cont.)*

Ten in a Den

Directions:

1. Distribute the handout on page 30.
2. Instruct the students to work individually, in pairs, or in groups to complete the handout.
3. Explain to the students that they should use their flip books to help them finish the words written on the bear's honey pots.
4. Then, have the students circle the words that rhyme with the word *den*.
5. Have the students practice reading the words that they wrote.

Answer Key: Answers will vary. See the Short E Word List for possible answers.

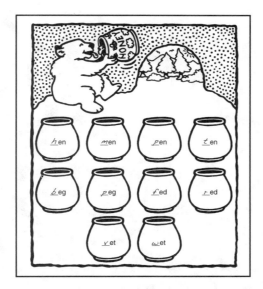

Wet Words

Directions:

1. Distribute the handout on page 31.
2. Instruct the students to work individually, in pairs, or in groups to complete the handout.
3. Explain to the students that they should use their flip books to help them finish the words inside of the fishbowl.
4. Then, have the students place an X over the words that do not rhyme with the word *wet*.
5. Have the students practice reading the words that they wrote.

Answer Key: Answers may include:

bet, get, jet, let, met, net, pet, set, vet, wet

beg, leg, peg

Caught in a Net

Directions: Use your flip books to help you finish the words that were caught in the net. Circle the words that rhyme with *net*.

28

Eggs

Directions: Use your flip books to finish the words inside of the eggs. Then, draw lines from the mother hen to the words that rhyme with *hen*.

Ten in a Den

Directions: Use your flip books to finish the words written on the bear's honey pots. Then, circle the words that rhyme with *den*.

Wet Words

Directions: Use your flip books to help you finish the words inside of the fish bowl. Put an **X** over the word that does not rhyme with *wet*.

Short I Flip Book

Directions: Make a flip book for each of your students.

1. Copy pages 32–36.
2. Cut the strips out horizontally, using the dotted lines as a guide.
3. Staple the strips together where the staple marks are indicated.
4. Cut the boxes vertically, cutting only on the dotted lines. Make sure not to separate the squares at the top.

staple	staple
b	in

staple	staple
d	ip

Short I Flip Book *(cont.)*

staple	staple
f	it

staple	staple
h	

staple	staple
k	

Short I Flip Book *(cont.)*

staple	staple
l	

staple	staple
p	

staple	staple
qu	

Short I Flip Book (cont.)

staple	staple
r	

staple	staple
s	

staple	staple
t	

Short I Flip Book (cont.)

staple	staple
W	

Short I Word List

Listed below are some words that can be made using the Short I Flip Book.

bin din fin pin	fit hit kit lit	dip hip lip rip
sin tin win bit	pit quit sit wit	sip tip

Activity Ideas for Teachers

The following activities can be used with the Short I Flip Book. Many of the activities have supporting materials. If the activities have supporting materials, the page numbers where the materials can be found will be provided.

══ Fins ══

Directions:

1. Distribute the handout on page 40.
2. Instruct the students to work individually, in pairs, or in groups to complete the handout.
3. Explain to the students that they should use their flip books to help them finish the words inside of the animals' fins.
4. Then, have the students place an **X** over the words that do not rhyme with the word fin.
5. Have the students practice reading the words that they wrote.

Answer Key: Answers may include:

bin, din, fin, pin, sin, tin, win

dip, hip, lip, rip, sip, tip

bit, fit, hit, kit, lit, pit, quit, sit, wit

══ Pick a Seat ══

Directions:

1. Before class, gather crayons, markers, or colored pencils.
2. During class, distribute the handout on page 41.
3. Instruct the students to work individually to complete the handout.
4. Explain to the students that they should use their flip books to help them finish the words inside of each chair.
5. Then, have the students circle and color their favorite chairs.
6. Have the students practice reading the words that they wrote.

Answer Key: Answers may include:

bit, fit, hit, kit, lit, pit, quit, sit, wit

Activity Ideas for Teachers *(cont.)*

Doctor's Kit

Directions:

1. Distribute the handout on page 42.
2. Instruct the students to work individually, in pairs, or in groups to complete the handout.
3. Explain to the students that they should use their flip books to help them finish the words inside of the doctor's kits.
4. Have the students practice reading the words that they wrote.

Answer Key: Answers may include:

bit, fit, hit, kit, lit, pit, quit, sit, wit

Vegetable Dip

Directions:

1. Distribute the handout on page 43.
2. Instruct the students to work individually, in pairs, or in groups to complete the handout.
3. Explain to the students that they should use their flip books to help them finish the words inside of the vegetables.
4. Then, have the students circle their favorite vegetables.
5. Have the students practice reading the words that they wrote.

Answer Key: Answers may include:

dip, hip, lip, rip, sip, tip

Short Vowels

Fins

Directions: Use your flip books to help you finish the words on each animal's fin. Then, place an **X** over the two fins that do not rhyme with the word *fin*.

Pick a Seat

Directions: Use your flip books to help you finish the words inside each chair. Then, circle and color your favorite chair.

Doctor's Kit

Directions: Use your flip books to help you finish the words inside of the doctor's kit.

Vegetable Dip

Directions: Use your flip books to help you finish the words inside of each vegetable. Circle your favorite vegetable.

Short O Flip Book

Directions: Make a flip book for each of your students.

1. Copy pages 44–48.
2. Cut the strips out horizontally, using the dotted lines as a guide.
3. Staple the strips together where the staple marks are indicated.
4. Cut the boxes vertically, cutting only on the dotted lines. Make sure not to separate the squares at the top.

staple	staple
c	ob

staple	staple
d	od

Short O Flip Book *(cont.)*

staple	staple
f	og

staple	staple
g	op

staple	staple
h	ot

Short O Flip Book *(cont.)*

staple	staple
j	

staple	staple
l	

staple	staple
m	

Short O Flip Book *(cont.)*

staple	staple
n	

staple	staple
p	

staple	staple
r	

Short O Flip Book *(cont.)*

staple	staple
S	

staple	staple
t	

Short O Word List

Listed below are some words that can be made using the Short O Flip Book.

cob	sob	rod	jog	mop
job	cod	sod	log	pop
mob	nod	fog	cop	top
rob	pod	hog	hop	

cot	hot	not
dot	jot	pot
got	lot	rot

Activity Ideas for Teachers

The following activities can be used with the Short O Flip Book. Many of the activities have supporting materials. If the activities have supporting materials, the page numbers where the materials can be found will be provided.

Dots

Directions:

1. Distribute the handout on page 53.
2. Instruct the students to work individually, in pairs, or in groups to complete the handout.
3. Explain to the students that they should use their flip books to help them finish the words inside of the dots.
4. Then, have the students place an **X** over the words that do not rhyme with the word *dot*.
5. Have the students practice reading the words that they wrote.

Answer Key: Answers may include:

cot, dot, got, hot, jot, lot, not, pot, rot
fog, hog, log, jog
cop, hop, mop, pop, top

Cut it Out!

Directions:

1. Before class, gather scissors and glue.
2. During class, distribute the handout on page 54.
3. Instruct the students to work individually to complete the handout.
4. Explain to the students that they should use their flip books to help them finish the words inside of items that belong to the police officer.
5. Then, have the students cut out the items, and glue them onto the person on the page.
6. Have the students practice reading the words that they wrote.

Answer Key: Answers may include:

cop, hop, mop, pop, top

Activity Ideas for Teachers *(cont.)*

Unhappy Clown

Directions:

1. Distribute the handout on page 55.
2. Instruct the students to work individually, in pairs, or in groups to complete the handout.
3. Explain to the students that they should use their flip books to help them finish the words inside of the clown's tears.
4. Have the students practice reading the words that they wrote.

Answer Key: Answers may include:
cob, job, mob, rob, sob

Frogs on a Log

Directions:

1. Distribute the handout on page 56.
2. Instruct the students to work individually, in pairs, or in groups to complete the handout.
3. Explain to the students that they should use their flip books to help them finish the words inside of the frogs.
4. Have the students practice reading the words that they wrote.

Answer Key: Answers may include:
fog, hog, log, jog

Activity Ideas for Teachers *(cont.)*

Peas in a Pod

Directions:

1. Distribute the handout on page 57.
2. Instruct the students to work individually, in pairs, or in groups to complete the handout.
3. Explain to the students that they should use their flip books to help them finish the words inside of the peas in the pod.
4. Have the students practice reading the words that they wrote.

Answer Key: Answers may include:

cod, nod, pod, rod, sod

Popcorn Display

Directions:

1. Before class, cut out the popcorn container on page 58.
2. Display the popcorn container on a bulletin board, large poster board, or other display area.
3. Gather scissors for the students to use.
4. During class, distribute the handouts on pages 58–63 to your students. There are five different handouts. Each individual student should complete at least one of the five different handouts.
5. Instruct the students to work individually to complete his/her assigned handout.
6. Explain to the students that they should use their flip books to help them finish the word inside of the piece of popcorn. After completing the word, each student should write his/her name inside the piece of popcorn. Then, each student should cut out the piece of popcorn.
7. Display the students' completed popcorn pieces in and around the popcorn container.

Answer Key:

Answers will vary. See the Short O Word List for possible answers.

Dots

Directions: Use your flip books to help you finish the words inside of the dots. Place an **X** over the words that don't rhyme with *dot*.

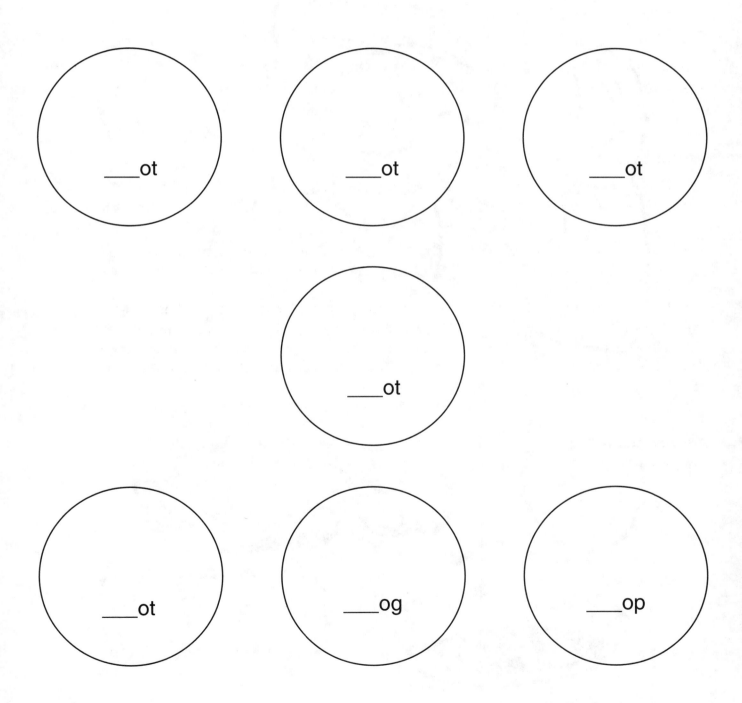

Cut it Out!

Directions: Use your flip books to help you finish the words inside the items that belong to the police officer. Then, cut out the items and glue them in the correct places.

Unhappy Clown

Directions: This clown is sobbing! Use your flip books to help you finish the words inside of the clown's tears.

Frogs on a Log

Directions: Use your flip books to help you finish the words inside of the frogs.

56

Peas in a Pod

Directions: Use your flip books to help you finish the words inside of the peas in the pod.

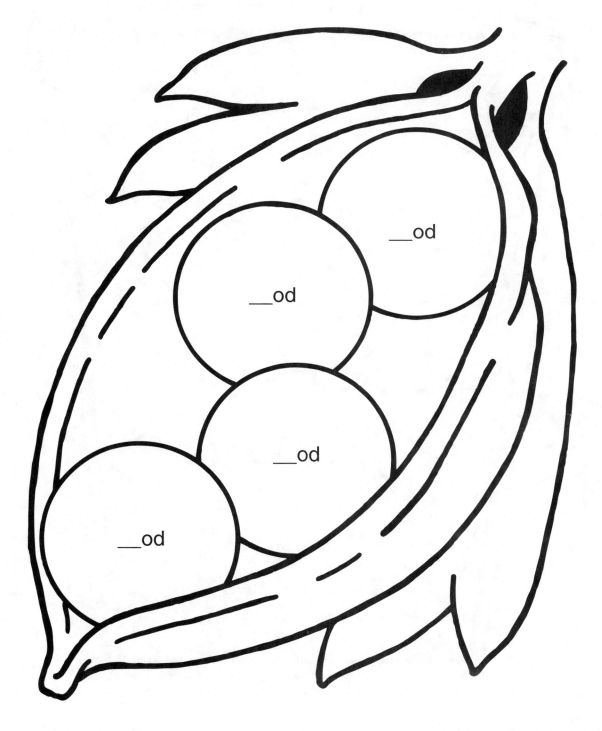

Popcorn Displays

Directions: Cut along the dotted line to cut out the popcorn container.

58

Popcorn
Display #1

Directions: Use your flip book to help you finish the word inside of the popcorn. Write your name inside the popcorn. Then, cut out the popcorn.

__ob

Name:_____

Popcorn
Display #2

Directions: Use your flip book to help you finish the word inside of the popcorn. Write your name inside the popcorn. Then, cut out the popcorn.

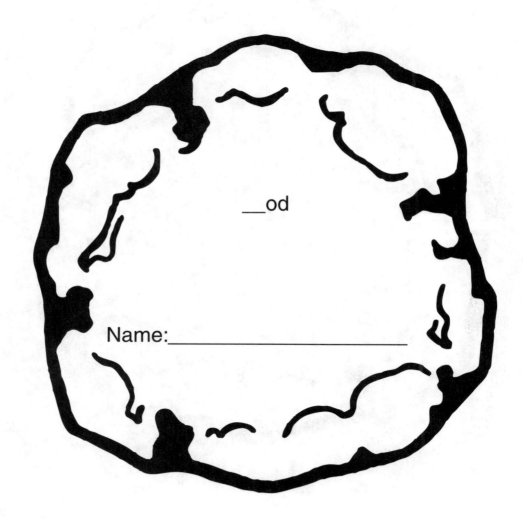

__od

Name:_____

60

Popcorn
Display #3

Directions: Use your flip book to help you finish the word inside of the popcorn. Write your name inside the popcorn. Then, cut out the popcorn.

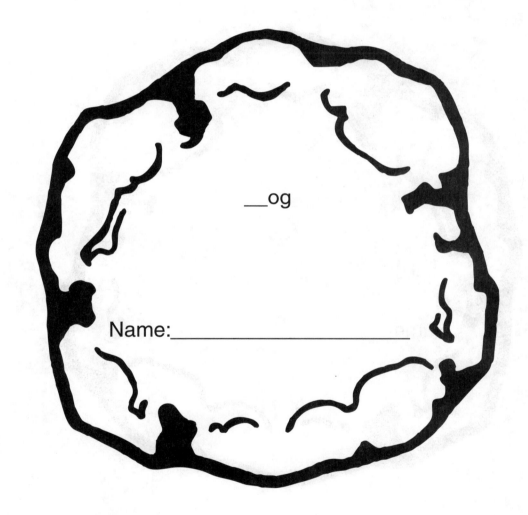

__og

Name:_____

Popcorn
Display #4

Directions: Use your flip book to help you finish the word inside of the popcorn. Write your name inside the popcorn. Then, cut out the popcorn.

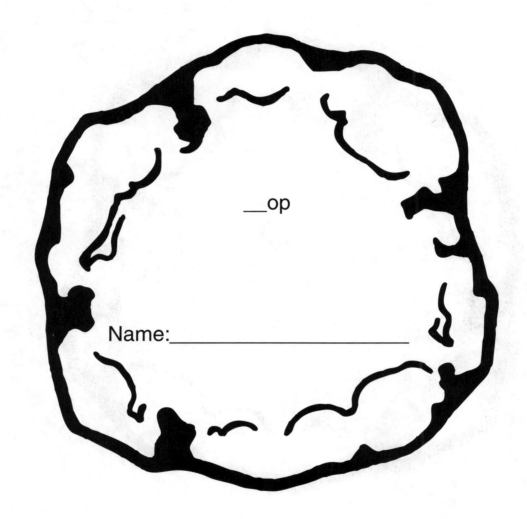

___op

Name:_____

Popcorn
Display #5

Directions: Use your flip book to help you finish the word inside of the popcorn. Write your name inside the popcorn. Then, cut out the popcorn.

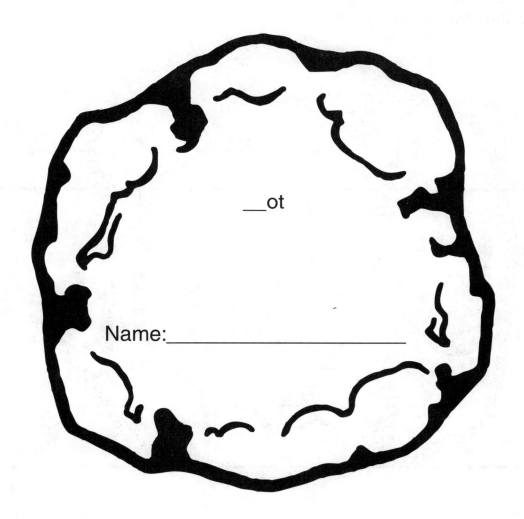

___ot

Name:_____

Short U Flip Book

Directions: Make a flip book for each of your students.

1. Copy pages 64–66.
2. Cut the strips out horizontally, using the dotted lines as a guide.
3. Staple the strips together where the staple marks are indicated.
4. Cut the boxes vertically, cutting only on the dotted lines. Make sure not to separate the squares at the top.

staple	staple
b	ub

staple	staple
c	ug

Short U Flip Book *(cont.)*

staple	staple
h	um

staple	staple
m	un

staple	staple
r	up

Short U Flip Book *(cont.)*

staple	staple
S	US

staple	staple
t	ut

Short U Word List

Listed below are some words that can be made using the Short U Flip Book.

bug
bun
bus
but

cub
cup
cut
hub

hug
hum
hut
mug

rub
rug
run
rut

sub
sun
tub
tug

Activity Ideas for Teachers

The following activities can be used with the Short U Flip Book. Many of the activities have supporting materials. If the activities have supporting materials, the page numbers where the materials can be found will be provided.

Fun Time with Rhymes

Directions:

1. Before class, cut out the Rhyme Time Cards (pages 71–72) and the Rhyme Time Smiles (page 73).
2. During class, instruct the students to use their flip books to make words that rhyme with words that you show them.
3. Explain to the students that when they show you a correct rhyming word, you will hand them a Rhyme Time Smile.
4. One at a time, hold up the Rhyme Time Cards. Remind the students to use their flip books to make a word that rhymes with the word that you are showing them. Say the word aloud.
5. As the students make rhyming words, hand them their Rhyme Time Smiles.

Answer Key: Answers may include:

club: cub, hub, rub, sub

dug: bug, hug, mug, rug, tug

gum: hum

fun: bun, run, sun

pup: cup

nut: but, cut, hut, rut

Tugboats

Directions:

1. Distribute the handout on page 74.
2. Instruct the students to work individually, in pairs, or in groups to complete the handout.
3. Explain to the students that they should use their flip books to help them finish the words that the tugboats are pulling.
4. Have the students practice reading the words that they wrote.

Answer Key: Answers may include:

tug, bug, hug, mug, rug, cub

Activity Ideas for Teachers *(cont.)*

Submarine Boats

Directions:

1. Distribute the handout on page 75.
2. Instruct the students to work individually, in pairs, or in groups to complete the handout.
3. Explain to the students that they should use their flip books to help them finish the words that are written on the submarine boats.
4. Have the students practice reading the words that they wrote.

Answer Key: Answers may include:

cub, hub, rub, sub

Buzzing Bees

Directions:

1. Distribute the handout on page 76.
2. Instruct the students to work individually, in pairs, or in groups to complete the handout.
3. Explain to the students that they should use their flip books to help them finish the words that are written on the buzzing bees.
4. Have the students practice reading the words that they wrote.

Answer Key: Answers may include:

bug, bun, bus, but

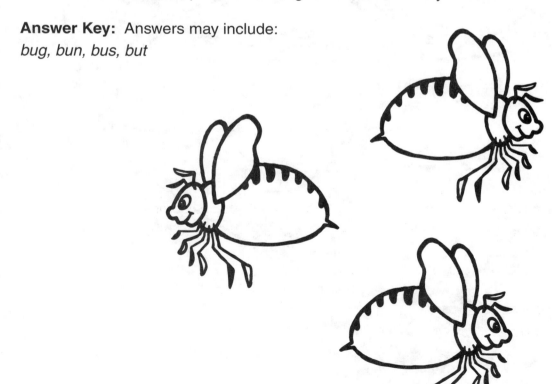

Activity Ideas for Teachers *(cont.)*

Magic Rug Ride

Directions:

1. Distribute the handout on page 77.
2. Instruct the students to work individually, in pairs, or in groups to complete the handout.
3. Explain to the students that they should use their flip books to help them finish the words that are written on the lamps riding on the magic rug.
4. Have the students practice reading the words that they wrote.

Answer Key: Answers may include:

rub, rug, run, rut

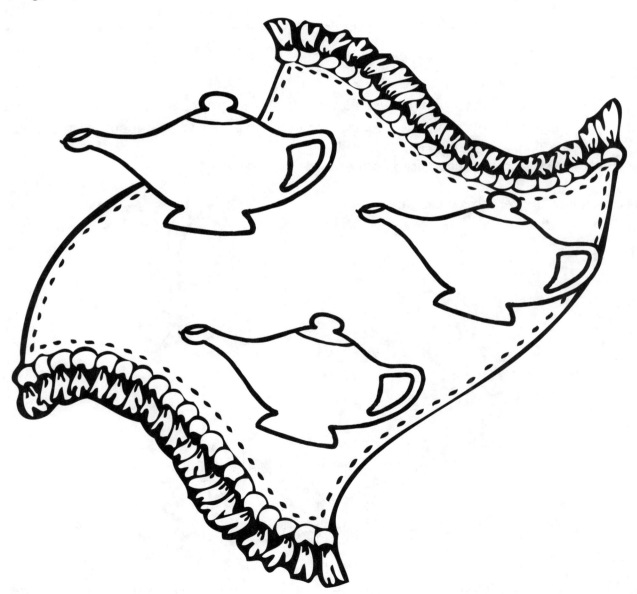

Fun Time with Rhymes

Directions: Before class, cut out the Rhyme Time cards.

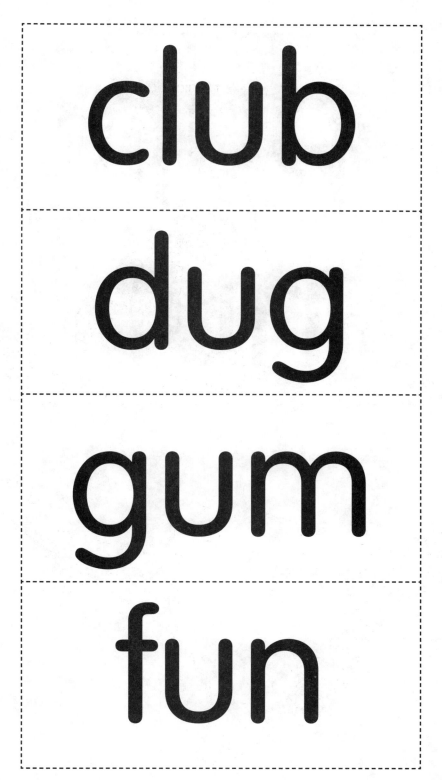

Fun Time with Rhymes *(cont.)*

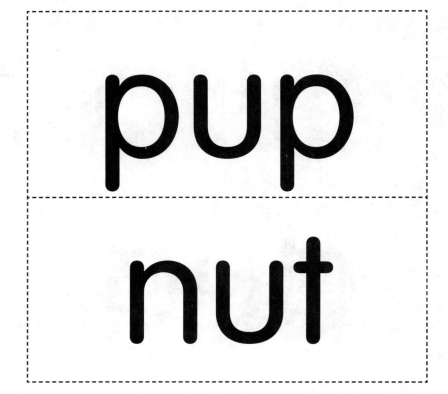

72

Fun Time with Rhymes *(cont.)*

Directions: If possible, copy onto colored paper. Then, before class, cut out the Rhyme Time Smiles for your students.

Tugboats

Directions: Use your flip books to help you finish the words that these tugboats are tugging.

_____ug

_____ug

_____ug

74

Submarine Boats

Directions: Use your flip books to help you finish the words that are written on the submarine boats.

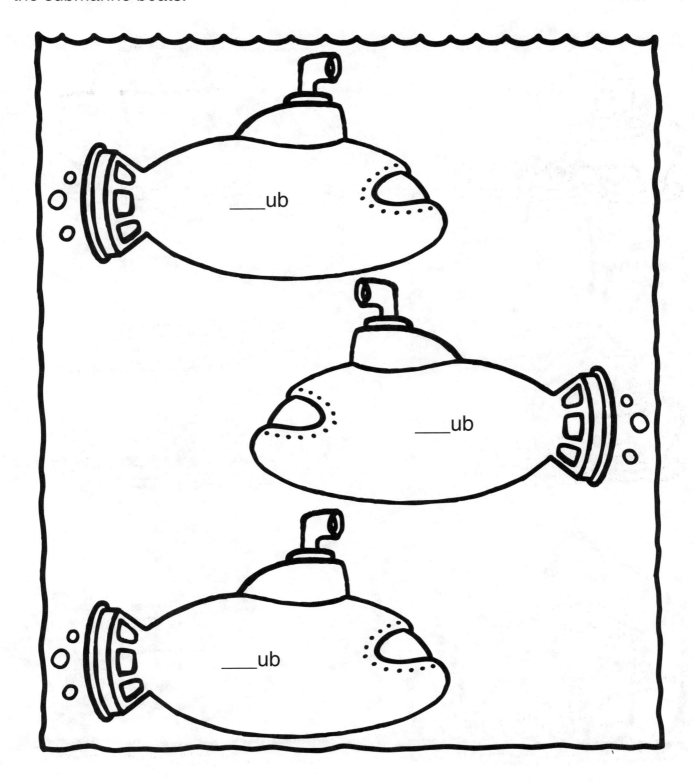

___ub

___ub

___ub

Buzzing Bees

Directions: Use your flip books to help you finish the words that are written on the buzzing bees.

Magic Rug Ride

Directions: Use your flip books to finish the words that are going for a ride on the flying rug.

A-E-I-O-U Flip Book

Directions: Make a flip book for each of your students.

1. Copy pages 78–79.

2. Cut the strips out horizontally, using the dotted lines as a guide.

3. Staple the strips together where the staple marks are indicated.

4. Cut the boxes vertically, cutting only on the dotted lines. Make sure not to separate the squares at the top.

staple	staple	staple
b	a	d

staple	staple	staple
h	e	g

A-E-I-O-U Flip Book *(cont.)*

staple	staple	staple
l	i	m

staple	staple	staple
p	o	n

staple	staple	staple
r	u	t

A-E-I-O-U Word List

Listed below are some words that can be made using the A-E-I-O-U Flip Book.

bad	bag	bug	bat	had	ham
bed	beg	ban	bet	hid	hem
bid	big	bin	bit	hag	
bug	bog	bun	but	hug	

him	hit	lad	lag	let	peg	pet
hum	hot	led	leg	lit	pig	pit
hat	hut	lid	log	lot	pat	pot

Activity Ideas for Teachers

Ladybug Spots

Directions:

1. Distribute the handout on page 83.
2. Instruct the students to work individually, in pairs, or in groups to complete the handout.
3. Explain to the students that they should use their flip books to help them finish the words inside the ladybug's spots.
4. Have the students practice reading the words that they wrote.

Answer Key:

bag, beg, big, bog, bug

Sleepy Words

Directions:

1. Distribute the handout on page 84.
2. Instruct the students to work individually, in pairs, or in groups to complete the handout.
3. Explain to the students that they should use their flip books to help them finish the words in the beds.
4. Have the students practice reading the words that they wrote.

Answer Key:

bad, bed, bid, bud

Activity Ideas for Teachers *(cont.)*

Floating Words

Directions:

1. Distribute the handout on page 85.
2. Instruct the students to work individually, in pairs, or in groups to complete the handout.
3. Explain to the students that they should use their flip books to help them finish the words on the hot air balloons.
4. Have the students practice reading the words that they wrote.

Answer Key:

hat, hit, hot, hut

Bats!

Directions:

1. Distribute the handout on page 86.
2. Instruct the students to work individually, in pairs, or in groups to complete the handout.
3. Explain to the students that they should use their flip books to help them finish the words that the bats are holding.
4. Have the students practice reading the words that they wrote.

Answer Key:

bat, bet, bit, but

Ladybug Spots

Directions: Use your flip books to help you finish the words in the ladybug's spots.

Sleepy Words

Directions: Use your flip books to help you finish the words that are in the beds.

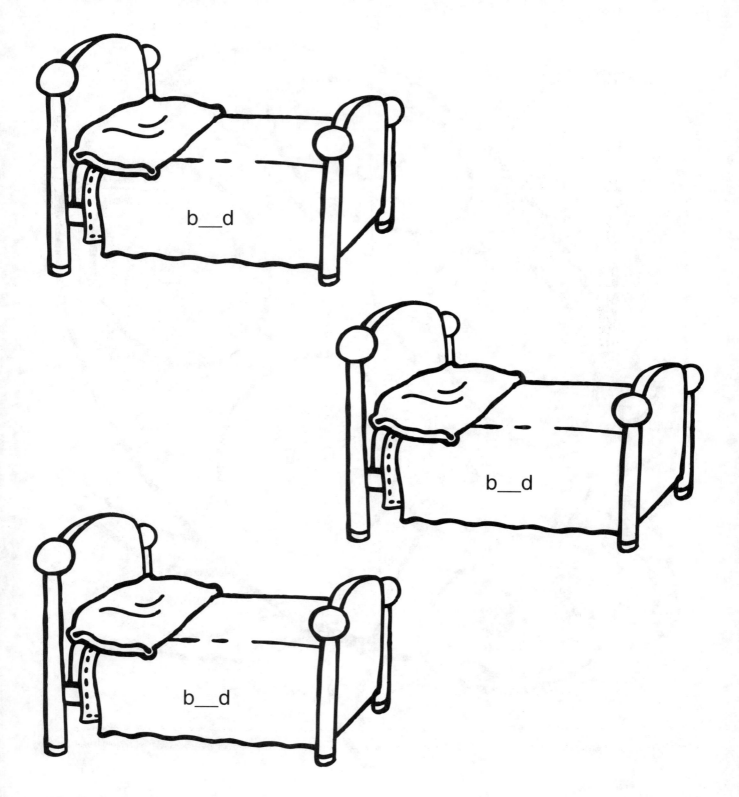

b__d

b__d

b__d

84

Floating Words

Directions: Use your flip books to help you finish the words that are floating on the hot air balloons.

Bats!

Directions: Use your flip books to help you finish the words that these bats are holding.

86

Long A Flip Book

Directions: Make a flip book for each of your students.

1. Copy pages 87–90.
2. Cut the strips out horizontally, using the dotted lines as a guide.
3. Staple the strips together where the staple marks are indicated.
4. Cut the boxes vertically, cutting only on the dotted lines. Make sure not to separate the squares at the top.

staple	staple
b	ace

staple	staple
c	aid

Long A Flip Book *(cont.)*

staple	staple
f	ake

staple	staple
g	ame

staple	staple
l	ain

88

Long A Flip Book *(cont.)*

staple	staple
m	ait

staple	staple
p	ape

staple	staple
s	ase

Long A Flip Book *(cont.)*

staple	staple
t	ate

staple	staple
w	ave

Long A Word List

Listed below are some words that can be made using the Long A Flip Book.

face
lace

bait
wait

cape
tape

cage
page
sage
wage

bake
cake
fake
lake

fate
gate
late

maid
paid

make
take
wake

gave
pave
save
wave

gain
main
pain

came
fame
game
same
tame

Activity Ideas for Teachers

The following activities can be used with the Long A Flip Book. Many of the activities have supporting materials. If the activities have supporting materials, the page numbers where the materials can be found will be provided.

Stand and Sit

Directions:

1. Instruct the students to stand.
2. Explain to the students that they should use their flip books to make a word with the Long A vowel sound.
3. Have the students show you the word that they made.
4. If the word is correct, have the student sit.
5. Continue until all the students are sitting down.

Answer Key:

Answers will vary. Use the Long A Word List on page 91 for possible answers.

Five-layered Cake

Directions:

1. Distribute the handout on page 94.
2. Instruct the students to work individually, in pairs, or in groups to complete the handout.
3. Explain to the students that they should use their flip books to help them finish the words inside the layers on the cake.
4. Have the students practice reading the words that they wrote.

Answer Key: Answers may include:

bake, cake, fake, lake, make, take, wake

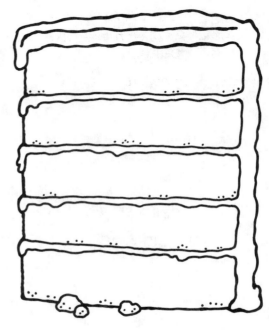

Activity Ideas for Teachers *(cont.)*

Save Your Money

Directions:

1. Distribute the handout on page 95.
2. Instruct the students to work individually, in pairs, or in groups to complete the handout.
3. Explain to the students that they should use their flip books to help them finish the words inside of the coins.
4. Have the students practice reading the words that they wrote.

Answer Key: Answers may include:

gave, pave, wave, save

Swan Lake Displays

Directions:

1. Before class, cut out the five different swan handouts on pages 96–100.
2. Create a "lake" using blue paper on a bulletin board or other display area.
3. During class, instruct the students to work in small groups to complete their assigned swan handout.
4. Explain to the students that they should use their flip books to help them finish the words inside of their swans. After completing the words, each student should place their swan in the "lake."

Answer Key:

cage, page, sage, wage
maid, paid, gain, main, pain, bait, wait
bake, cake, fake, lake, make, take, wake
gave, pave, wave, save
came, fame, game, same, tame

Five-layered Cake

Directions: Use your flip books to help you complete the words inside each layer of the cake.

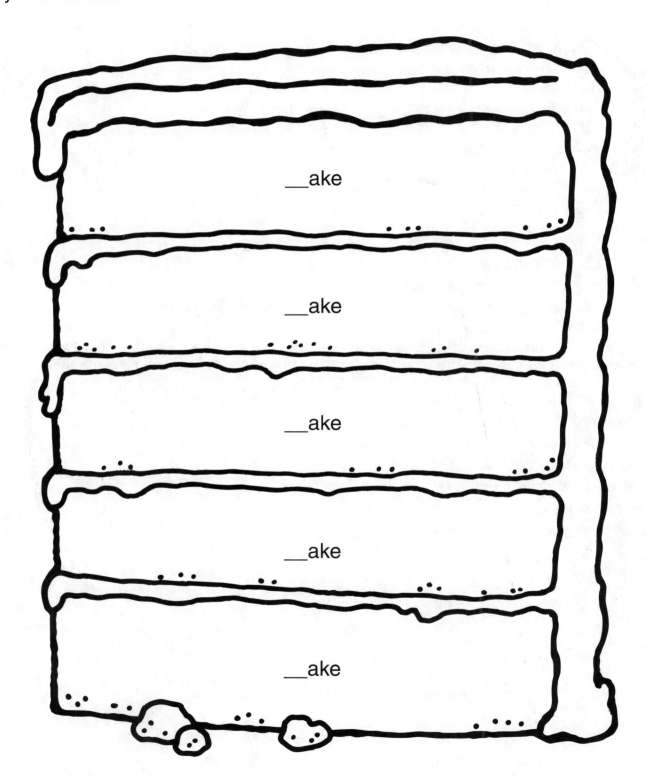

Save Your Money

Directions: Use your flip books to help you finish the words in the coins.

Swan Lake
Display #1

Directions: Before class, copy and cut out the swan.

Swan Lake
Display #2

Directions: Before class, copy and cut out the swan.

__ai__

__ai__

Swan Lake
Display #3

Directions: Before class, copy and cut out the swan.

__ake

__ake

__ake

98

Swan Lake
Display #4

Directions: Before class, copy and cut out the swan.

__ __ve

__ __ve

__ __ ve

Swan Lake
Display #5

Directions: Before class, copy and cut out the swan.

__ame

__ame

__ame

100

Long E Flip Book

Directions: Make a flip book for each of your students.

1. Copy pages 101–104.
2. Cut the strips out horizontally, using the dotted lines as a guide.
3. Staple the strips together where the staple marks are indicated.
4. Cut the boxes vertically, cutting only on the dotted lines. Make sure not to separate the squares at the top.

staple	staple
b	**ead**

staple	staple
d	**eed**

Long E Flip Book (cont.)

staple	staple
f	eaf

staple	staple
h	eef

staple	staple
l	eak

Long E Flip Book (cont.)

staple	staple
m	eek

staple	staple
n	eal

staple	staple
p	eel

Long E Flip Book *(cont.)*

staple	staple
r	eat

staple	staple
s	eet

Long E Word List

Listed below are some words that can be made using the Long E Flip Book.

bead
deed
feed
heed
lead
need
reed
read
seed

leek
leak
meek
peak
peek
seek

beat
beet
feat
feet
heat
meat
meet
neat
seat

beef
leaf
beak

deal
feel
heel
meal
peal
real
reel
seal

Activity Ideas for Teachers

The following activities can be used with the Long E Flip Book. Many of the activities have supporting materials. If the activities have supporting materials, the page numbers where the materials can be found will be provided.

─────────────────────── **Seals** ───────────────────────

Directions:

1. Distribute the handout on page 109.
2. Instruct the students to work individually, in pairs, or in groups to complete the handout.
3. Explain to the students that they should use their flip books to help them finish the words inside the balls that the seals are balancing.
4. Have the students practice reading the words that they wrote.

Answer Key: Answers may include:

bead, lead, read, leaf, beak, leak, peak, deal, meal, peal, real, seal, beat, feat, heal, meat, neat

─────────────────────── **Feed the Birds** ───────────────────────

Directions:

1. Distribute the handout on page 110.
2. Instruct the students to work individually, in pairs, or in groups to complete the handout.
3. Explain to the students that they should use their flip books to help them finish the words on the birdfeeders.
4. Have the students practice reading the words that they wrote.

Answer Key: Answers may include:

deed, feed, heed, need, reed, seed, beef, leek, peek, meek, seek, feel, heel, reel, beet, feet

Activity Ideas for Teachers *(cont.)*

Feet

Directions:

1. Before class, gather unlined paper.
2. During class, instruct the students to trace their feet on the paper.
3. Explain to the students that they should use their flip books to help them write words that have a Long E vowel sound in their feet, like the word *feet.*
4. Have the students practice reading the words that they wrote.

Answer Key:

Answers may vary. See the Long E Word List on page 105 for possible answers.

High-heeled Shoes

Directions:

1. Distribute the handout on page 111.
2. Instruct the students to work individually, in pairs, or in groups to complete the handout.
3. Explain to the students that they should use their flip books to help them finish the words inside the shoes' heels.
4. Have the students practice reading the words that they wrote.

Answer Key: Answers may include:

deal, feel, heel, meal, peal, real, reel, seal

Activity Ideas for Teachers *(cont.)*

Words You Can Read

Directions:

1. Distribute the handout on page 112.
2. Instruct the students to work individually, in pairs, or in groups to complete the handout.
3. Explain to the students that they should use their flip books to help them finish the words inside of the award ribbons.
4. Have the students practice reading the words that they wrote.

Answer Key: Answers may include:

bead, lead, read

leaf

beak, leak, peak

deal, meal, peal, real, seal

Seals

Directions: Use your flip books to help you finish the words inside of the balls that the seals are balancing.

Feed the Birds

Directions: Use your flip books to help you finish the words on the bird feeders.

110

High-heeled Shoes

Directions: Use your flip books to help you finish the words inside the shoes' heels.

__eel

__eal

__eel

__eel

__eal

__eal

__eal

__eal

Words You Can Read

Directions: Use your flip books to complete the words inside the award ribbons.

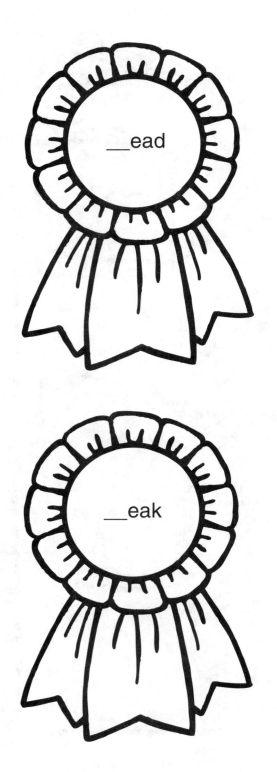

__ead

__eak

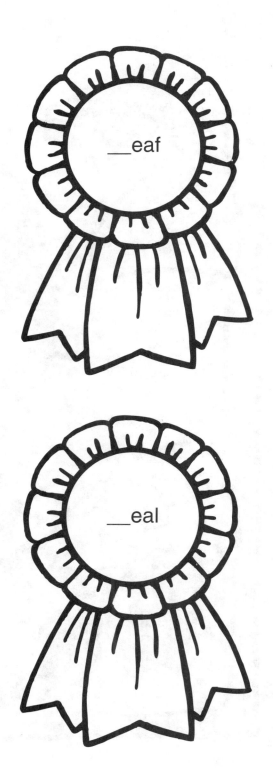

__eaf

__eal

Long I Flip Book

Directions: Make a flip book for each of your students.

1. Copy pages 113–116.
2. Cut the strips out horizontally, using the dotted lines as a guide.
3. Staple the strips together where the staple marks are indicated.
4. Cut the boxes vertically, cutting only on the dotted lines. Make sure not to separate the squares at the top.

staple	staple
b	ice

staple	staple
h	ide

Long I Flip Book *(cont.)*

staple	staple
k	ife

staple	staple
l	ike

staple	staple
m	ile

Long I Flip Book *(cont.)*

staple	staple
p	**ite**

staple	staple
r	

staple	staple
s	

Long I Flip Book *(cont.)*

staple	staple
t	

staple	staple
w	

Long I Word List

Listed below are some words that can be made using the Long I Flip Book.

lice
mice
rice

life
wife

mile
pile
tile

hide
ride
side
wide

bike
hike
like
pike

bite
kite
site

Activity Ideas for Teachers

The following activities can be used with the Long I Flip Book. Many of the activities have supporting materials. If the activities have supporting materials, the page numbers where the materials can be found will be provided.

━━━━━━━━━━━━━━━━━━━━━ **Fly a Kite** ━━━━━━━━━━━━━━━━━━━━━

Directions:

1. Distribute the handout on page 120.
2. Instruct the students to work individually, in pairs, or in groups to complete the handout.
3. Explain to the students that they should use their flip books to help them finish the words inside of the kites.
4. Then, ask the students to circle the words that rhyme with the word *kite*.
5. Have the students practice reading the words that they wrote.

Answer Key: Answers may include:

bite , kite , site

bike, hike, like, pike

━━━━━━━━━━━━━━━━━━━━━ **I Like You** ━━━━━━━━━━━━━━━━━━━━━

Directions:

1. Distribute the handout on page 121.
2. Instruct the students to work individually, in pairs, or in groups to complete the handout.
3. Explain to the students that they should use their flip books to help them finish the words inside of the hearts.
4. Have the students practice reading the words that they wrote.

Answer Key: Answers may include:

lice, mice, rice

bike, like, hike, pike

mile, pile, tile

Activity Ideas for Teachers *(cont.)*

─────────────────────── **Ice Land** ───────────────────────

Directions:

1. Distribute the handout on page 122.
2. Instruct the students to work individually, in pairs, or in groups to complete the handout.
3. Explain to the students that they should use their flip books to help them finish the words inside of the penguins' bellies.
4. Then, ask the students to circle the words that rhyme with the word *ice*.
5. Have the students practice reading the words that they wrote.

Answer Key: Answers may include:

(lice), (mice), (rice)

life, wife

bike, like, hike, pike

─────────────────────── **Tokens** ───────────────────────

Directions:

1. Before class, cut out the flashcards and tokens on pages 123–125. Each team can earn up to eight tokens.
2. During class, place the students into small groups.
3. Explain to the students that you will show them some flashcards. The group of students should use a flip book to finish the words that describe the pictures on the flashcards. Once the words are written, the groups should hold up their flip books for you to see.
4. As the groups show the correct answers, award them with tokens. See how many tokens each group can earn.

Answer Key:

mice, rice, hide, ride, wife, bike, pile, bite

Fly a Kite

Directions: Use your flip books to help you finish the words inside of the kites. Circle the words that rhyme with the word *kite*.

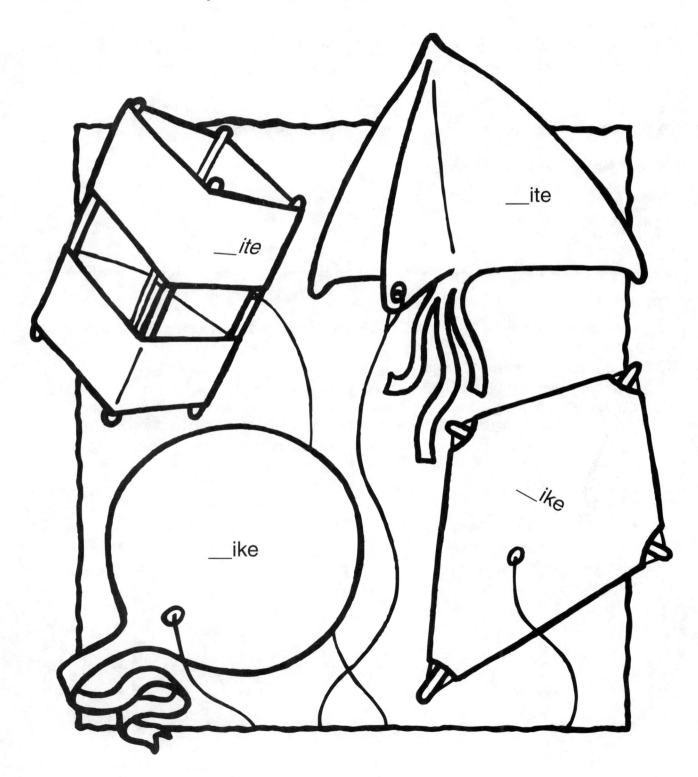

I Like You

Directions: Use your flip books to help you finish the words inside of the hearts.

Ice Land

Directions: Use your flip books to help you finish the words inside of the penguins' bellies. Circle the words that rhyme with the word *ice*.

Tokens

Directions: Before class, cut out the flashcards.

___ice

___ice

___ide

___ide

Tokens *(cont.)*

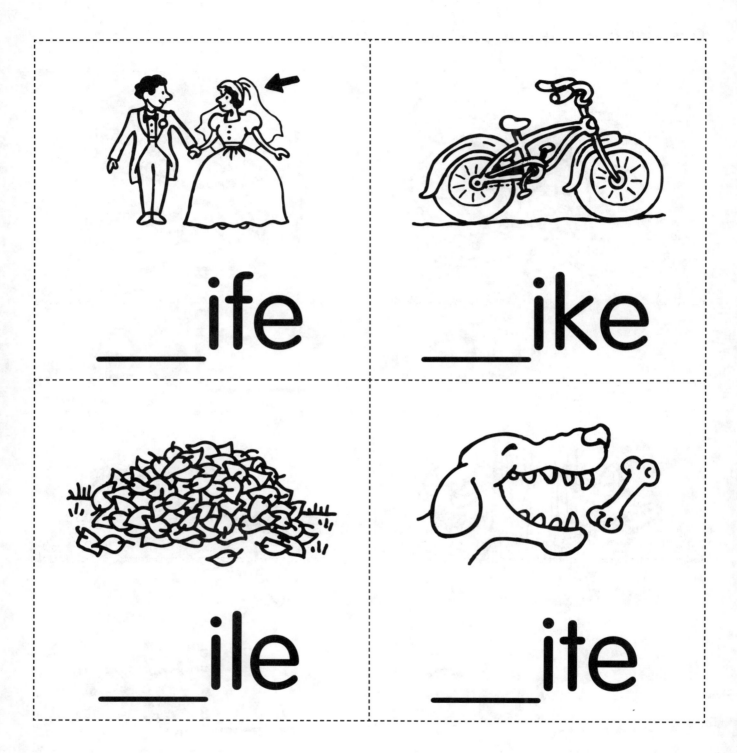

___ife

___ike

___ile

___ite

Tokens *(cont.)*

Directions: Before class, cut out the tokens.

Long O Flip Book

Directions: Make a flip book for each of your students.

1. Copy pages 126–129.
2. Cut the strips out horizontally, using the dotted lines as a guide.
3. Staple the strips together where the staple marks are indicated.
4. Cut the boxes vertically, cutting only on the dotted lines. Make sure not to separate the squares at the top.

staple	staple
b	oad

staple	staple
c	oaf

Long O Flip Book *(cont.)*

staple	staple
d	oat

staple	staple
g	obe

staple	staple
h	ome

Long O Flip Book *(cont.)*

staple	staple
l	**ope**

staple	staple
m	

staple	staple
r	

Long O Flip Book (cont.)

staple	staple
t	

Long O Word List

Listed below are some words that can be made using the Long O Flip Book.

boat
coat
goat
moat

dome
home

cope
hope
mope
rope

load
road
toad

loaf

Activity Ideas for Teachers

The following activities can be used with the Long O Flip Book. Many of the activities have supporting materials. If the activities have supporting materials, the page numbers where the materials can be found will be provided.

═══════════════════════ **Tasty Os** ═══════════════════════

Directions:

1. Distribute the handout on page 133.
2. Instruct the students to work individually, in pairs, or in groups to complete the handout.
3. Explain to the students that they should use their flip books to help them finish the words inside of the circles.
4. Have the students practice reading the words that they wrote.

Answer Key: Answers may include:

boat, coat, goat, load, loaf, moat, road, toad

═══════════════════════ **Ropes** ═══════════════════════

Directions:

1. Distribute the handout on page 134.
2. Instruct the students to work individually, in pairs, or in groups to complete the handout.
3. Explain to the students that they should use their flip books to help them finish the words inside of the loops in the rope.
4. Then, have the students circle the word that does not rhyme with the word *rope*.
5. Have the students practice reading the words that they wrote.

Answer Key: Answers may include:

cope, hope, mope, rope
(home), (dome)

Activity Ideas for Teachers *(cont.)*

Soap Bubbles

Directions:

1. Distribute the handout on page 135.
2. Instruct the students to work individually, in pairs, or in groups to complete the handout.
3. Explain to the students that they should use their flip books to help them finish the words inside of the bubbles.
4. Have the students practice reading the words that they wrote.

Answer Key: Answers may include:

boat, coat, goat, load, loaf, moat, road, toad

Toad Road

Directions:

1. Before class, gather some tape and cut out a toad for each student (page 136).
2. Then, draw a road on the chalkboard or on a large piece of paper.
3. During class, distribute a toad to each student.
4. Instruct the students to use their flip books to help them write a word with a long o vowel sound inside of their toads.
5. Once the students have written their words inside of their toads, have the students tape their toads in the road.
6. Have the students practice reading the words on the toad road.

Answer Key:

Answers will vary. See the Long O Word List on page 130 for possible answers.

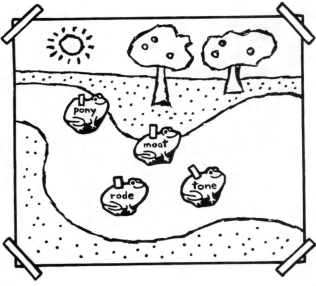

Tasty Os

Directions: Use your flip books to help you finish the words inside of the Tasty Os.

Ropes

Directions: Use your flip books to help you finish the words on the page. Circle the words that do not rhyme with the word *rope*.

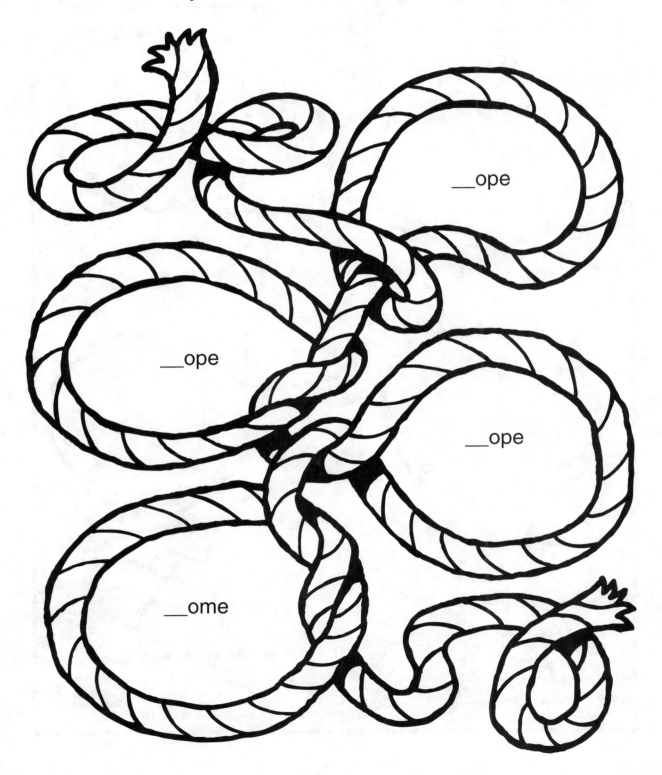

134

Soap Bubbles

Directions: Use your flip books to help you finish the words inside of the bubbles.

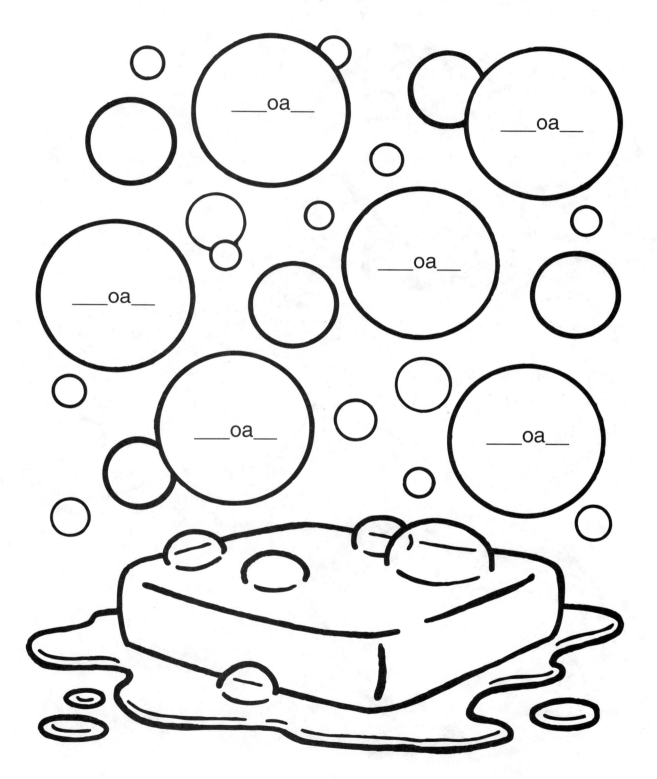

Toad Road

Directions: Cut out a toad for each student.

Long U Flip Book

Directions: Make a flip book for each of your students.

1. Copy pages 137–139.

2. Cut the strips out horizontally, using the dotted lines as a guide.

3. Staple the strips together where the staple marks are indicated.

4. Cut the boxes vertically, cutting only on the dotted lines. Make sure not to separate the squares at the top.

staple	staple
c	ube

staple	staple
d	ule

Long U Flip Book (cont.)

staple	staple
fl	une

staple	staple
gl	ute

staple	staple
m	ue

138

Long U Flip Book *(cont.)*

staple	staple
S	

staple	staple
t	

staple	staple
tr	

Long U Word List

Listed below are some words that can be made using the Long U Flip Book.

cube
tube

dune
tune

cue
flue
glue
sue
true

mule
rule

cute
mute
flute

Activity Ideas for Teachers

The following activities can be used with the Long U Flip Book. Many of the activities have supporting materials. If the activities have supporting materials, the page numbers where the materials can be found will be provided.

Build-a-Suit

Directions:

1. Before class, cut out the parts of the suit on pages 142–148. Each student should get at least one part of the suit.
2. During class, give each student a suit part.
3. Instruct the students to use their flip books to help them finish the word on their piece of clothing.
4. Have the students color their article of clothing.
5. Put the different parts of the suits together, and display them around the room.
6. Have the students practice reading the words that they wrote.

Answer Key:

Answers will vary. See the Long U Word List on page 140 for possible answers.

Tunes

Directions:

1. Distribute the handout on page 149.
2. Instruct the students to work individually, in pairs, or in groups to complete the handout.
3. Explain to the students that they should use their flip books to help them finish the words inside of the music notes.
4. Have the students practice reading the words that they wrote.

Answer Key:

Answers will vary. See the Long U Word List on page 140 for possible answers.

Build-a-Suit

Directions: Use your flip books to help you finish the word on the tie.

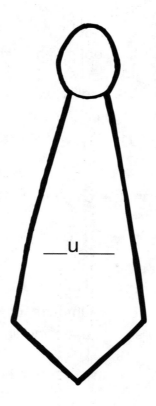

__u___

Build-a-Suit *(cont.)*

Directions: Use your flip books to help you finish the word on the shirt.

__u__

Build-a-Suit *(cont.)*

Directions: Use your flip books to help you finish the word on the jacket.

144

Build-a-Suit *(cont.)*

Directions: Use your flip books to help you finish the word on the pants.

__u__

Build-a-Suit *(cont.)*

Directions: Use your flip books to help you finish the word on the belt.

Build-a-Suit (cont.)

Directions: Use your flip books to help you finish the word on the shoe.

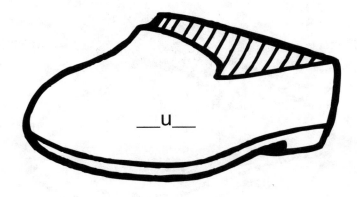

__u__

Build-a-Suit *(cont.)*

Directions: Use your flip books to help you finish the word on the shoe.

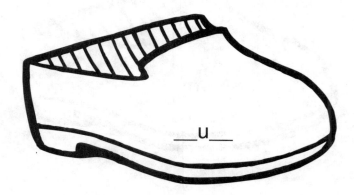

Tunes

Directions: Use your flip books to help you finish the words inside of the music notes.

Ending Word Patterns Flip Book I

Directions: Make a flip book for each of your students.

1. Copy pages 150–154.
2. Cut the strips out horizontally, using the dotted lines as a guide.
3. Staple the strips together where the staple marks are indicated.
4. Cut the boxes vertically, cutting only on the dotted lines. Make sure not to separate the squares at the top.

staple   staple

b   all

staple   staple

c   ent

Ending Word Patterns Flip Book I *(cont.)*

staple	staple
d	ind

staple	staple
f	old

staple	staple
g	ung

Ending Word Patterns Flip Book I *(cont.)*

staple	staple
h	

staple	staple
k	

staple	staple
l	

Ending Word Patterns Flip Book I *(cont.)*

staple	staple
m	

staple	staple
r	

staple	staple
s	

Ending Word Patterns Flip Book I *(cont.)*

staple	staple
t	

staple	staple
v	

staple	staple
w	

Ending Word Patterns Word List I

Listed below are some words that can be made using the Ending Word Patterns
Flip Book I.

ball
call
fall
hall
mall
tall
wall

bind

bold
cold
fold
gold
hold
mold
sold

bent
cent
dent
lent
rent
sent
tent
vent
went

find
hind
kind
mind
rind
wind

hung
lung
rung
sung

Activity Ideas for Teachers

The following activities can be used with the Ending Word Patterns Flip Book I. Many of the activities have supporting materials. If the activities have supporting materials, the page numbers where the materials can be found will be provided.

Wind Chimes

Directions:

1. Distribute the handout on page 159.
2. Instruct the students to work individually, in pairs, or in groups to complete the handout.
3. Explain to the students that they should use their flip books to help them finish the words inside of the wind chimes. Point out that the word "wind" can be read with a short and a long "I."
4. Have the students practice reading the words that they wrote.

Answer Key:

bind, find, hind, kind, mind, rind, wind

Word Wall

Directions:

1. Distribute the handout on page 160.
2. Instruct the students to work individually, in pairs, or in groups to complete the handout.
3. Explain to the students that they should use their flip books to help them finish the words that are written on the word wall.
4. Have the students practice reading the words that they wrote.

Answer Key:

ball, call, fall, hall, mall, tall, wall

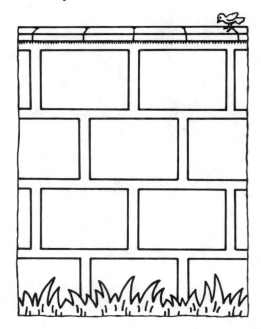

Activity Ideas for Teachers *(cont.)*

Gold Nuggets

Directions:

1. Distribute the handout on page 161.
2. Instruct the students to work individually, in pairs, or in groups to complete the handout.
3. Explain to the students that they should use their flip books to help them finish the words inside of the gold nuggets.
4. Have the students practice reading the words that they wrote.

Answer Key:

bold, cold, fold, gold, hold, mold, sold

Hung Out to Dry

Directions:

1. Distribute the handout on page 162.
2. Instruct the students to work individually, in pairs, or in groups to complete the handout.
3. Explain to the students that they should use their flip books to help them finish the words inside of the clothing that have been hung out to dry.
4. Have the students circle the words that rhyme with the word *hung*.

Answer Key: Answers may vary.

(lung), (rung), (sung)

ball, call, fall, hall, mall, tall, wall

Activity Ideas for Teachers *(cont.)*

Sent with Love

Directions:

1. Distribute the handout on page 163.
2. Instruct the students to work individually, in pairs, or in groups to complete the handout.
3. Explain to the students that they should use their flip books to help them finish the words inside of the envelopes.
4. Have the students practice reading the words that they wrote.

Answer Key:

bent, cent, dent, lent, rent, sent, tent, vent, went

Wind Chimes

Directions: Use your flip books to help you finish the words with long I vowel sounds in the wind chime.

Word Wall

Directions: Use your flip books to help you finish the words on the word wall.

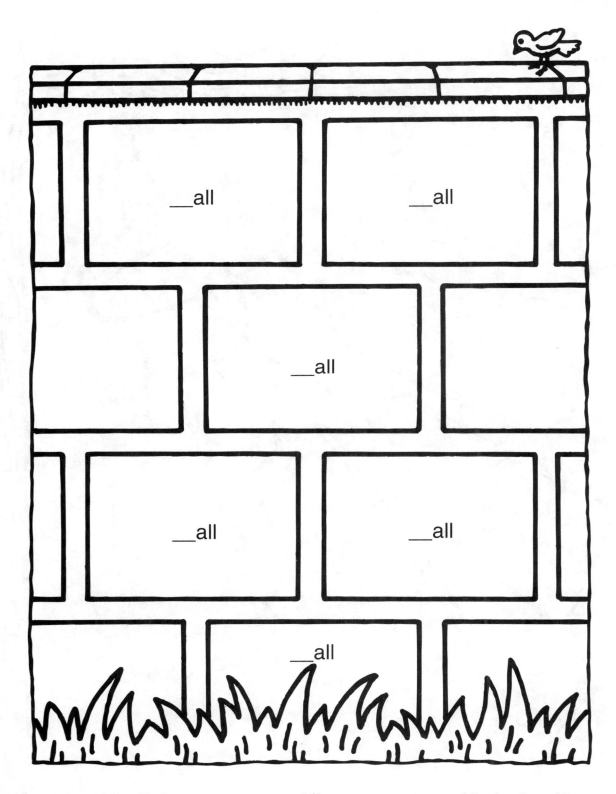

Gold Nuggets

Directions: Use your flip book to help you finish the words inside of the gold nuggets.

Hung Out to Dry

Directions: Use your flip books to help you finish the words inside of the clothes that have been hung out to dry. Circle the words that rhyme with *hung*.

___ung

___ung

___ung

___ung

___all

Sent with Love

Directions: Use your flip books to help you finish the words inside of the envelopes.

Ending Word Patterns
Flip Book II

Directions: Make a flip book for each of your students.

1. Copy pages 164–168.

2. Cut the strips out horizontally, using the dotted lines as a guide.

3. Staple the strips together where the staple marks are indicated.

4. Cut the boxes vertically, cutting only on the dotted lines. Make sure not to separate the squares at the top.

staple	staple
b	ail

staple	staple
c	eat

Ending Word Patterns Flip Book II *(cont.)*

staple	staple
d	ill

staple	staple
f	oil

staple	staple
g	

Ending Word Patterns Flip Book II *(cont.)*

staple	staple
h	

staple	staple
m	

staple	staple
n	

Ending Word Patterns Flip Book II *(cont.)*

staple	staple
p	

staple	staple
s	

staple	staple
t	

Ending Word Patterns Flip Book II *(cont.)*

staple	staple
W	

168

Ending Word Patterns Word List II

Listed below are some words that can be made using the Ending Word Patterns Flip Book II.

bail	beat	bill	boil
fail	feat	dill	coil
hail	heat	fill	foil
mail	meat	gill	soil
nail	neat	hill	toil
pail	seat	mill	
sail		pill	
tail		sill	
wail		till	
		will	

Activity Ideas for Teachers

The following activities can be used with the Ending Word Patterns Flip Book II. Many of the activities have supporting materials. If the activities have supporting materials, the page numbers where the materials can be found will be provided.

Shovels and Pails

Directions:

1. Distribute the handout on page 173.
2. Instruct the students to work individually, in pairs, or in groups to complete the handout.
3. Explain to the students that they should use their flip books to help them finish the words on the side of the pails.
4. Have the students practice reading the words that they wrote.

Answer Key:

bail, fail, hail, mail, nail, pail, sail, tail, wail

Fill the Page

Directions:

1. Distribute the handout on page 174.
2. Instruct the students to work individually, in pairs, or in groups to complete the handout.
3. Explain to the students that they should use their flip books to help them make words.
4. Once the students are finished making words, lead them through the rest of the directions. Instruct the students to circle a word that rhymes with *snail*, put a rectablge around a word that rhymes with *treat*, put a triangle around a word that rhymes with *spill*, and draw an oval around a word that rhymes with *spoil*.

Answer Key: Answers will vary.

See the Ending Word Patterns Word List II on page 169 for possible answers.

Activity Ideas for Teachers *(cont.)*

Snakes that Coil

Directions:

1. Distribute the handout on page 175.
2. Instruct the students to work individually, in pairs, or in groups to complete the handout.
3. Explain to the students that they should use their flip books to help them finish the words inside of the snakes.
4. Have the students practice reading the words that they wrote.

Answer Key:

boil, coil, foil, soil, toil

Game: Take a Seat

Directions:

1. Tell the students that they will be playing a game, and that they will each need a flip book.
2. Explain to the students that they will shut their eyes and flip their flip books to a word. When you say open, the students should then open their eyes.
3. When the students' eyes are open, they should look at their flip books. If the students have made a real word, they should remain standing. All other students should take a seat.
4. Teachers may wish to continue the game until only one student remains standing, or teachers may wish to just start the game over each time so that all students are always engaged.

Activity Ideas for Teachers *(cont.)*

Tails

Directions:

1. Distribute the handout on page 176.
2. Instruct the students to work individually, in pairs, or in groups to complete the handout.
3. Explain to the students that they should use their flip books to help them finish the words on the tails of the animals.
4. Have the students practice reading the words that they wrote.

Answer Key:

bail, fail, hail, mail, nail, pail, sail, tail, wail

Shovels and Pails

Directions: Use your flip books to help you finish the words written on the side of the pails.

__ail   __ail

__ail   __ail

Fill the Page

Directions: What words can you make using your flip books? Write them in the box below.

Circle a word that rhymes with (*snail*).

Put a rectangle around a word that rhymes with | *treat* |.

Put a triangle around a word that rhymes with *spill*.

Draw an oval around a word that rhymes with *spoil*.

Snakes that Coil

Directions: Use your flip books to help you finish the words written on the snakes.

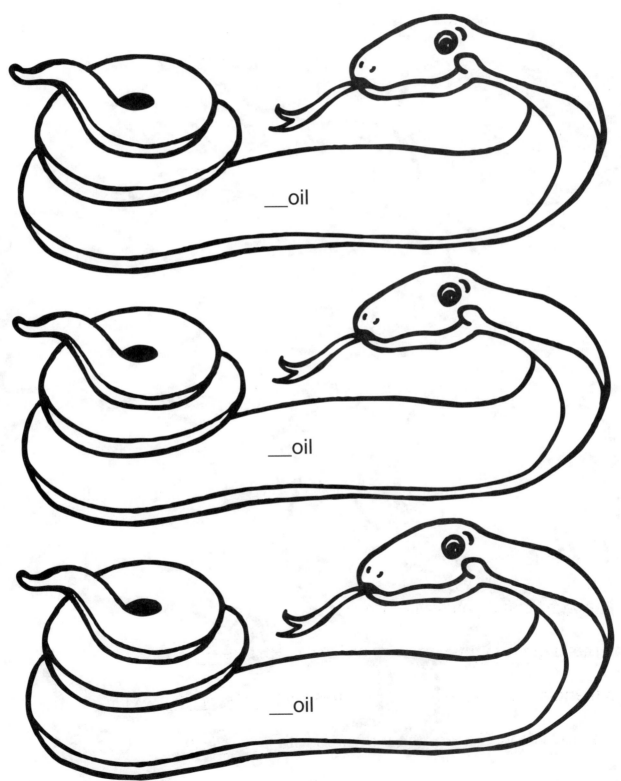

__oil

__oil

__oil

Tails

Directions: Use your flip books to help you finish the words on the animals' tails.

__ail

__ail

__ail

__ail